Squalus acanthias

Zachary Webb Nicholls

I0116358

The sale of this book without a front cover is unauthorized. If this book is sold without a cover, then the author and the publishing company may have not received payment for it.

Squalus acanthias

Copyright © 2016 by Zachary Webb Nicholls (a.k.a Dr. Jaws)

All rights reserved. Published in the United States by Deep Sea Publishing LLC, Herndon, Virginia.

This is a work of fiction. Names, characters, places, and incidents either are the product of the author's imagination or are used fictionally. Any resemblance to actual persons, living or dead, events or locales is entirely coincidental.

ISBN-13: 978-1-939535-18-4
ISBN: 1939535182
E-Book ISBN-13: 978-1-939535-19-1
E-Book ISBN: 1939535190

www.deepseapublishing.com

Printed in the United States of America

Hello friend,

What you are about to read is secret.

Each word, picture, and symbol has a meaning, and together they will help you find something very strange, but very exciting. Furthermore, each word, picture, and symbol is anchored in a living truth, but in order to fully understand what that truth is, you need to do some exploring.

Beyond this little book, there is a boundless, bountiful wealth of knowledge within your reach. You of course are not required to seek it, but if you do, I assure you will be rewarded with a richer understanding of our shark, the seas, and the mystery of life itself.

For now, you hold in your hands a map. Let it take you—from the past, to the present, to the weird—deep into an ocean of legends, of dark wonders, and of amber eyes…

….let it take you to Shark.

Starlight is finite
A star has a time to end
Explosive its death

Scattered star pieces
Combine into the combined
Birth of sun and earth

Sun fire creates
With calm earth, air, and
water
Life elemental

~ *Domain Eukarya* ~

Imagine a mountain

Cool and calming

Trickling water down its slope

It is serene in its grey

Paint it with a domain

Of life so rich in color

That the eyes will forever wonder

At its design and sustain

A curiosity

Unique only to Eukarya

When cell within cell became cell itself

So long ago, a peak

In life was reached

From origins so humble

Came oranges so fiery

With jades, emeralds, and harlequins each

Beauties of the forest

Protecting the ambling reds

And boisterous blues

With calming arms best

Suited for shading

Amber-centered violets

And cinnabar-sighted mosaics

All art never fading

This domain is of color

See Eukarya

Splendid and diverse

Muses of the world

For the art that it is

~*Kingdom Animalia*~

Look what the dawn has broken

Something new stirs in the seas

A novel language now spoken

The animals have come to be

~

From one tiny sponge to one funny man

A simple life will always be banned

A drama that we cannot understand

The animals, come and play, come and play

A hardworking ant meets an unfriendly beetle

While two birds romance, it seems nothing's sweeter

A seahorse's dance is such a unique love

Animals, come and play, come and play

~

Embrace the feeling of life

A body that's one from many

A hunger that sets you right

~

And chase in manner uncanny

Your strange sweet compassions

You animal, go and play, go and play

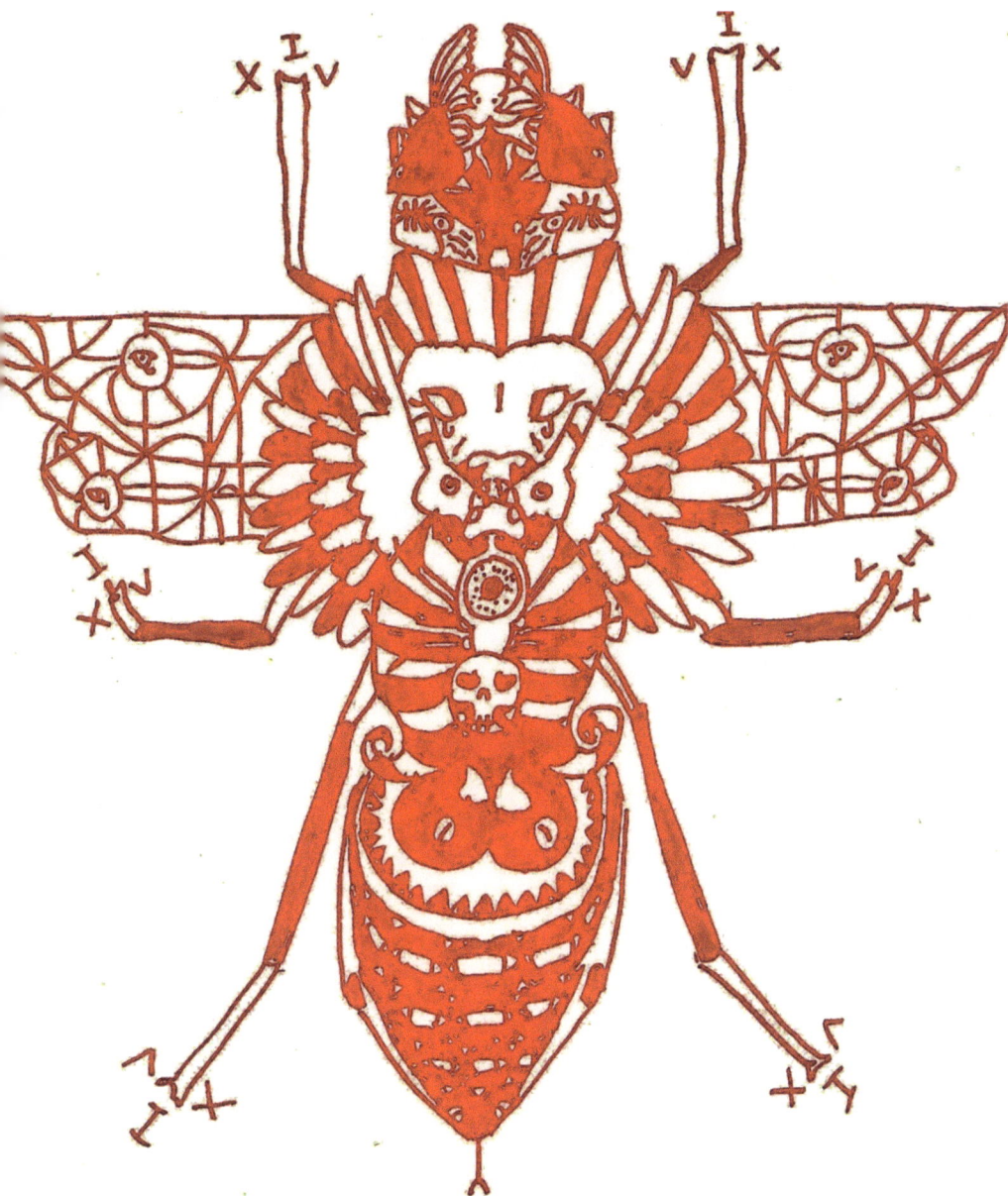

~Phylum Chordata~

CORD

BROTHERS & SISTERS

now is the time to change the game

we are for ph... related

but we are humanlike

BILATERAL

NOT

irvIEWvrs

CONG

in the HCE min

form OHR style

ROV

DRE

a t i o n

D a t a ...

~ *Class Chondrichthyes* ~

There is a hall of marble and limestone—of honor and ocean—adorned with obsidian shadows; the Chondrichthyan Silhouettes. Each Silhouette is an embodiment of form and essence, said to be constructed by the gods to remind the world of the Living Shadows; the chimaera, the ray, and the shark. Believed to be guardians of both the ocean and the human soul, The Living Shadows served to consume the weaknesses of each. Through so doing, they culled corruption and pro-tected the life of both soul and sea. To honor this nobility cloaked in ferocity, the Chondrichthyan Silhouettes are each adorned with an eye of pearl and gemstone. Together, body and eye capture the essence of a Living Shadow:

A power cooled with grace
An immortal who could die
A legend with a heartbeat.

~Order Squaliformes~

Downcast past the briny light

Emerge the bats of ocean's night
Beneath the dark of pearly tides
They gleam, their eyes fluorescent bright

Within the mists of their abyss
They tease their scales of amethyst
And though most shy with quandary naught
Some others probe with ashen lips

Pale hadal jaws bite from the seep
And charcoal fins writhe through the deep
But, lighting gloom with bellies blue,
Most to themselves with caution keep

Such prickly dogs of gracious gulp
And sleeping kites that seize the pulp
Ascend in schools electric teal
To lap the light of lunar bulb

But like the sun to poles enticed
They crave the climb towards tides of ice
For unlike sharks of warmer climes
With dark and cold, they are sufficed

~Family Squalidae ~

The dogfish sharks prime

In abundance and design

Spurn sharp their decline

~*Genus Squalus*~

SEA FISH

"Rbe aksucqb lpe rejlncktq; icrcjs rbecp jerq, qmelpcjs rbecp ucqbepq, rbey lpe rk ie qeej lq rbe hkqr aeucljr."

Note: The above is a keyword cypher. The keyword is hidden on the following page. Use it to unlock a smaller insight.

The Thorny One

Linnaeus, 1758

Squalus acanthias

A tiny shark with an average mass of 3kg. It is distinguished by its white spots and placement of the first dorsal fin behind the free rear tips of the pectoral fins.

Piked Dogfish   **Mielga**

أبوشوكة   白斑角鯊   アブラツノザメ

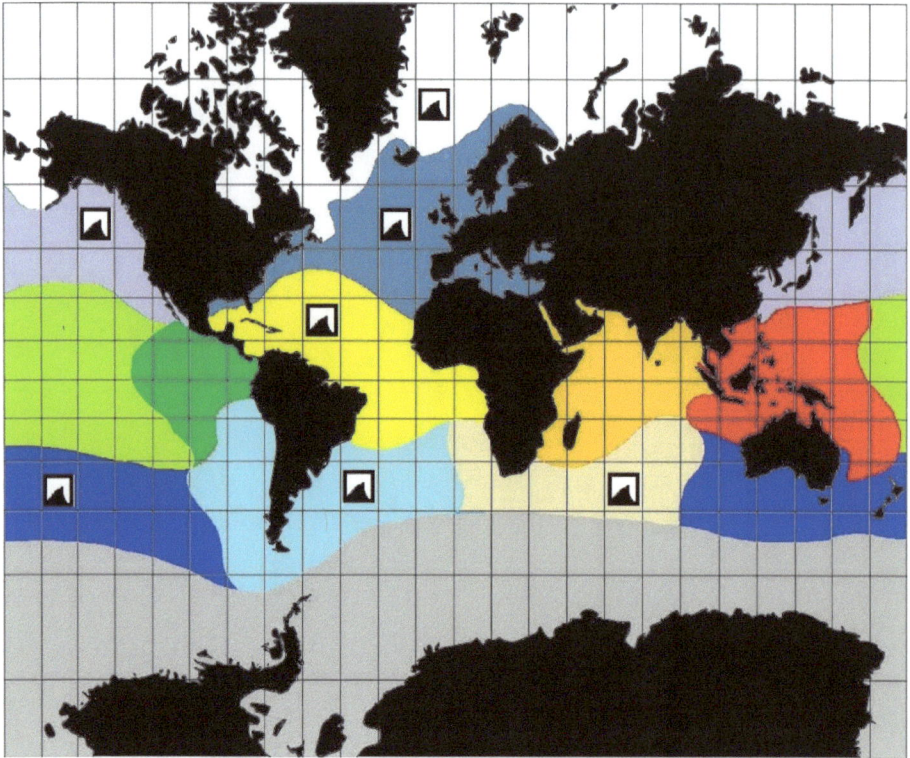

~*Global Distribution*~

North Akula Sea

Tempest Requin Sea

Wild Zame Sea

Sunset Sea of Reken

Colorful Sea of Sarka

Bountiful Sea of Shayu

Peaceful Sea of Mano

Sunrise Sea of Tiburon

Grande Tubarao Sea

Groot Haai Sea

Great Shark Sea

South Sarko Sea

~Haunts~

Squalus acanthias
can be found in the following zones:

Littoral   **Neritic**

Sunlit   **Twilight**

And the following special habitats:

Polar Seas

~

"We are one."

~ *Habits* ~

Squalus acanthias is perhaps the most well studied shark on the planet. The species has an infamously long pregnancy of about 2 years, and possesses an incredibly protracted lifespan of up to 100 years, according to some.

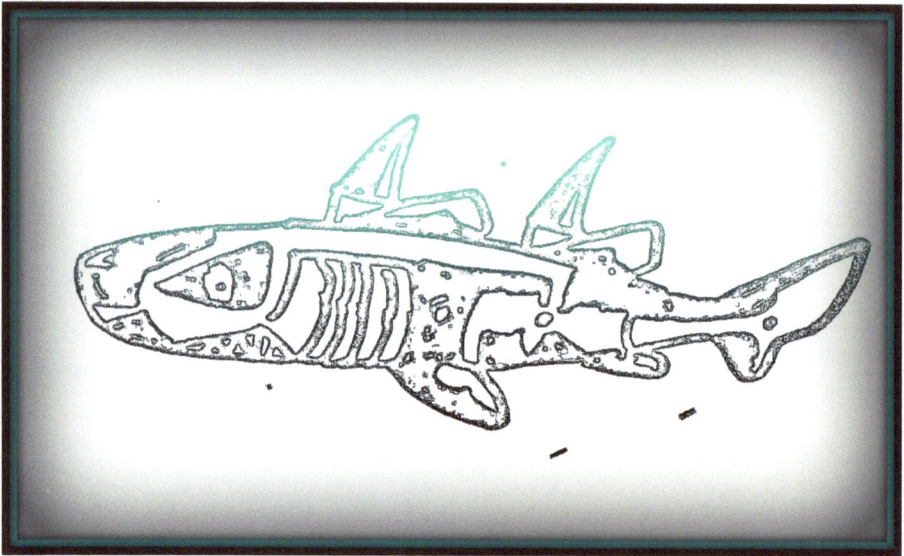

Squalus acanthias is famous for undertaking strong migrations and for schooling in great 'packs' segregated by sex and age. Packs of pregnant females are the most often caught by fishermen. Once captured, the shark is known to protest by chewing through nets and stabbing its handlers with mildly toxic dorsal spines.

~ *Humanity* ~

Squalus acanthias is to be perceived as a

HARMLESS SHARK

In light of the comforting attributes that follow;

Its tiny size

Its nonfatal poison

These attributes are presented with the truth that
Squalus acanthias has been implicated in

NO ATTACKS WHATSOEVER

As a resource, the species offers meat, oil, and leather, and is a
cornerstone of scientific literature and study on sharks

~

However, man has overfished *Squalus acanthias* and
has furthermore been responsible for damaging the
species' reproductive rate by targeting packs of large
pregnant females due to their size

As a result, *Squalus acanthias* is a

VULNERABLE SPECIES

~ Dark Moon Isle ~

"A tale about our shark, and yet much more..."

Night is where you found me...I call throughout the night...

Welcome to Dark Moon Isle. You are standing alone in a storm barely illuminated by the starlight; the rain seems to tire, and will not help you and your search for the key. Indeed, you must search…for you must unlock the Isle's trap….

First, you should perhaps gather some clues. The island is abandoned, and you seem to be the only soul here. Uncomfortably enough, you are alone on this small patch of Acadian rock currently pummeled by an icy rain and iron sea. The Isle is roughly circular and with little feature, save for an abandoned seafarer's cabin behind you. Though you should investigate, you sincerely don't want to approach the cabin. It doesn't feel right.

You instead want to move forward towards a jetty of towering boulders ahead. You begin to walk, but distinctly hear a soft cracking of brambles behind you. Take another step—there it is again: a step to match your step.

You should run..

Dashing across the prickly field, you finally arrive at a change in terrain; the brambles stop, and jagged rocks take their place. Your pace slows, and you carefully plant your feet into the dangerous grip of each rugged patch. As you progress further from the island's center, you realize that the footsteps behind you have ceased. Taking some comfort from this agreeable development, you make your way towards the larger boulders.

These precipices present more of a challenge as they are closer to the sea; they are more slippery and dangerous, and don't have many places to grip. You'd rather not scale them, but you have no choice; fear employs your animal nature, and compels you to summit each peak and claim its bleak horizon.

The seawater begins to take over.

Your feet get wet and terribly cold—the icy tide seems to be literally cutting into your flesh—but you must press on. There is not only something behind you, but also something around the corner...something pulling you in…

At last, the tallest peak of all is before you; you must climb it. The rotted seaweed shall serve as traction—a place to grip and become farther from danger—whilst the barnacles will create a menace with their shark-tooth casings. Keep climbing to the top and don't look back.

Don't look back.

Avoiding its craggy edges, you behold at the summit a horrific sight. Before you, the steely sea surrounds not only your peak, but also a ring of giant, terrifying statues below: awful figures of torment, contortion, and contrivance. Lying within the heart of the ring is a single, dark, unfathomable well.

Something is very wrong about this arrangement.

The storm stops. Clouds part directly above the well, and the moon—completely dark and defined only by a crisp, crimson outline— suddenly appears. At this particular instance, the supernatural emerges; the statues begin to cry tears of red—you hope to heaven it isn't blood—and slowly change their position. As the reddish sap descends, each statue raises a solemn hand. When the terribly sanguine fluid finally reaches the edge of the pool, the statues take cue, and point gravely downward into the heart of the well.

The cosmic is locked.

You.

Will.

Be.

Thrown.

In.

Without warning, without hope, you are pushed off of your peak, and approach, with the strongest of gravities, the iron face of dark moon well.

SURRENDER

Welcome to Dark Moon Isle.

You are somewhere beneath the island, but where exactly, you cannot say. A cloudy, crimson portal is above you, and you are completely submerged in a sea without temperature. You may breathe.

Looking around, you assume that this place is devoid of life. The portal's dim light barely illuminates a grand sphere of water surrounded by darkness, and you think nothing of monsters perhaps hiding in the shadows…at least not for now.

Rapidly, you descend. Against your will, you are pulled to the bottom; there's no use fighting it.

There is no order in this place.

There is no time here.

Abruptly, you collide with the seafloor. Though you may believe this to be a surreal circumstance, you feel a genuinely rough seabed composed of acutely edged grains and shell bits. Blood-red light gradually fills the arena, and betrays the presence of minute particles drifting within the water. Inexplicably, your vision becomes unnaturally enhanced, and you catch a magnified glimpse of the finer details of this particulate matter.

In one instance, you see an abundance of cells; some are whirling freely, while others are serving as food for larger, more complex designs. These latter creatures vary greatly in appearance, with either gigantic eyes, elongated spines, or polished claws serving as a their most significant feature. They are all plankton, the keystones of marine life, and they entice the appetite of millions.

A sudden burst of forage fish—herring, mackerel, and capelin—collides into the sphere. They douse your eyes as dark shadows blocking the red light, and career from edge-to-edge, creating a gloomy orbit of voracious predation. You count six different schools appearing and disappearing into the darkness; at times when you cannot see them, you still hear an incredibly thunderous chorus of scales breaking the water.

Perhaps also listening to this cacophony, two mantas—one white, one black—elegantly glide into the sphere of darkness. Each perfectly mirrors the other's flight, and both gently disrupt the six schools, one-by-one, taking only a small portion of fish as their own claims.

So goes the Plan.

This feast before you withholds something. Some secret is locked within: a hidden truth essential to your escape. It is a key of sorts, but it occurs with a guardian... a final school is coming.

You hear it first...a different pattern of scales. More silent, more spectral...a litheness in the water. You feel an electric chill that excites you, but you are still grounded by your reverence. You will be escorted by the otherworldly. Where to, you cannot say.

Enter the shark.

After a final pass between the two mantas, a single, tiny, but commanding shark enters the darkened sphere. It approaches from the seabed and ascends to meet you, ignoring the colossal globes of fish and the further feasts of the rays. Gravely, it wishes to intercept you. Bowing down in a request for guidance, you accept the arrival.

The shark first rises towards your head, processing behind topaz eyes the secrets you reveal with your own. It then encircles you, periodically moving from an orbit level with your head to one level with your toes. Another appears from an unseen vantage and creates a similar path. A third sharks form a larger circle with your waist as its center. A fourth does the same but sets your heart as its anchor.

Two more sharks join the group, but swim in a pattern much more cryptic than the other four. Their paths seem illogical, but deep within you know that there is something more to this…

Suddenly, the eyes and spots of all six sharks begin to glow. The blood-red sphere falls out of focus, and all you can see are the dancing lights in the dark. They begin to move away, but at a deliberately slow pace, and you solemnly follow.

The suspension of time is felt most strongly in the darkness.

Diligently following the lights before you, you overlook a collection of new, diminutive lamps emerging from beneath. As you continue to swim, they increase in number, until finally you realize that you can distinguish the sharks' dim outlines by the lights below…what are they? They almost look like…

Stars.

The sharks abruptly stop, and begin to swim in a circle, once again placing you at the center. With each shark's completion of its orbit, the submarine starlight grows stronger, until you can unmistakably see, beyond the bizarre ocean surface beneath you, the Milky Way and its constellations: Perseus, Cygnus, Gemini, Orion, Cetus, Pegasus…even Capricorn.

The most disturbing facet of this impossibility is the fact that you feel upright; the stars *should* be beneath you…but then what is above? As if to answer your question, the six sharks rise, and reveal with their lights a rocky ceiling rife with large holes and crags.

Deep purple sponges and ghost-white tunicates overwhelm the jagged face, and creeping spider crabs emerge from some holes only to once again disappear into others. Three of the sharks suddenly break protocol to dive into some of the tunnels, and reappear soon after with a new prize in their jaws: a slumbering moon snail with a peculiarly designed shell.

After ripping out the delectable body, a shark directly above you drops its shell, and you catch it. You examine the case intently, and discover odd symbols and lines, all arranged in a purposeful pattern.

It's a map.

Looking back at the porous ceiling, you realize in astonishment that it looks like a maze. There are seven possible entrances to choose from, and after consulting the curious map once again, you decide to choose the portal in the center, placed almost equidistantly from the other six entrances. As you hoist yourself into this dubious cavern, you fail to notice that the other six sharks are choosing their own gateways with a matched pace.

Three possible tunnels—one claustrophobic, one full of spider crabs, and one spacious and empty—are now before you. The map is inscribed with what appears to be a tiny crab claw; thus, you reluctantly choose the second tunnel. Though dark and constantly pulsating with its scurrying denizens, it is thankfully penetrated by small rocky windows to the starlight below.

You soon reach a choice that the map does not convey: a fork with two paths. The dark tunnel to your left lacks the many gaps and windows found in the light tunnel to your right. The former is deep, mysterious, but protected; the latter is illuminated, defined, but exposed. Exposure would not really have been a problem if you were alone…but there is something watching you.

From one of the smaller holes, you see two frightening developments; firstly, the distance between you and the starlit 'bottom' is shrinking. The heavens are moving closer, and though in some ways that may be comforting, the second observation—that the constellation Capricorn is, independently of its brethren, writhing its way towards you—dispels any sense of security. Though you cannot see Capricorn's eyes, you most definitely feel them, and thus choose to flee out of sight.

Enter the dark path.

Moving slowly, you worm your way through the twisting tunnel. Sometimes you feel the movement of unseen animals in the tunnel, skirting past your legs, your belly, and your back. It's indeed uncomfortable, but upon hearing what sounds like an echo of a roar from below, beyond the tunnel's walls, you affirm that this was the right choice. Ignorance is indeed bliss, you believe.

Finally, you arrive at a modest, carved chamber with a glassy floor. Beyond the barrier you can see that the stars are looming ever-closer, and that Capricorn has already transcended into your part of the sea: instead of a constellation, a gargantuan whale-like beast with a furrowed brow is circling beneath the glass.

It wants you.

Doing your best to ignore the titan below, you try to focus on the details of this cavern, for evidently, it is a special place. Looking up, you spy six arches supported by six different figures, each holding a key. Every pair of eyes is focused on the center of the chamber, but you see nothing. One of these keys must lead to escape…but which one?

As you cautiously approach the center, you see shadows emerge from the mouths of each statue. After they once-again ignite their spots and eyes, you realize that they're only the sharks from before. They begin to circle you once more and in a similarly odd pattern; however, you are now at full-attention, and are rather desperately trying to decipher the riddle that they present.

Two are head-to-toe. One is at your waist. Another is at your heart. Why are these important? What about the other two? What do they have to do with you?

Suddenly, the glass cracks.

No time left. You need to choose.

Ignoring the sharks, you frantically study the statues; they are all human, and look familiar to those tortured forms from before, except that this time they are more peaceful. Each of the six faces is unique in design, and you understand that they primarily convey one of six attributes: stability, creativity, power, love, thought, and intuition.

Which one is correct?

More cracks; the glass will break! Quickly!

You reach for the key that you trust in panic, but the minute you touch its colorless handle, the glass below shatters, and the monster roars. The six sharks dive down with spines arched, but surprisingly aim for the gigantic maw now rocketing upward.

One by one, each shark is swallowed, and nothing now separates you and the ascending beast. Instinctively, you dodge to the left and just barely miss its massive jaws: the leviathan continues upwards to only crash through the chamber ceiling. Upon Capricorn's impact, the entire maze collapses, and falls in pieces all around you.

But that is the least of your worries.

Looking below, you realize that the starry expanse is too hurtling upwards, and at is center is the same dark moon from before.

This collision you can't avoid.

Rapidly ascending, the black moon is ready to swallow both you and the monster. The rocks tumble around you, and the water begins to disintegrate. Moments before this final cosmic impact, amidst the immersive chaos, you find yourself pondering a strange last thought:

Was there a seventh option?

Wake.

You sit up. You find yourself lying in the middle of a small field of brambles. It is night, and cold rain is lightly falling upon your face. You glance left and spy an abandoned seafarer's cabin. You hear waves and other sounds of a nocturnal sea.

Rise.

Welcome to Dark Moon Isle. You are standing alone in a storm barely illuminated by the starlight; the rain seems to tire, and will not help you and your search for the key. Indeed, you must search...for you must unlock the Isle's trap.

Respect the seas and all who
call them home.

~ *Thanks* ~

To Christina Southard, who has been steadfastly loyal and supportive; thank you for your encouragement and friendship.

To Andy Murch, who possesses a plethora of powerful photos at Elasmodiver.com; thank you for your stunning shot of *Squalus acanthias* (page 21). It made all the difference.

To those who may be inspired, never trade your inspiration. You can be whomever you want; that choice is always yours. Keep seeking your higher being, and never let go of your love."

~*Zachary W. Nicholls*
The First Dr. Jaws

www.ingramcontent.com/pod-product-compliance
Lightning Source LLC
Chambersburg PA
CBHW041222270326
41933CB00001B/12